Today is Wesak. It's a special day. I'm making a lotus-flower light.

I am going with my friends to our temple. We'll float our lotus-flower lights on the river. The lights remind us of the Buddha, the prince who became a teacher. Today is the Buddha's birthday.

I'll tell you a story about him.

The Buddha's real name was Prince Siddhartha. His mother was Queen Maya. When Prince Siddhartha was born, a wise man told Queen Maya that her son was a special baby who would be a great teacher.

Prince Siddhartha grew up in the palace. He had everything he wanted – fine clothes and servants. His parents loved Siddhartha. They wanted him to stay in the palace for ever.

When he grew up, Siddhartha wanted to see what life was like outside the palace. He asked his servant, Channa, to take him to visit the town in his chariot.

On their first visit, Siddhartha saw an old man.

On their second visit, Siddhartha saw a sick man.

On their third visit, Siddhartha saw a dead man.

Siddhartha was surprised. He had never seen anyone look like this before. Channa told Siddhartha that everyone gets old and sick and dies.

Siddhartha felt sad when he remembered the old man, the sick man and the dead man. He wanted everyone to be young and healthy and happy for ever. He wanted everyone to live in a rich palace with fine clothes and servants. Thinking about these things made Siddhartha feel even more sad.

Then Siddhartha saw a monk dressed in a simple saffron robe and carrying a bowl to collect food.

The monk seemed calm and happy. He did not look sad like Siddhartha.

One night, when everyone was asleep, Prince Siddhartha left the palace. He put on a simple saffron robe like the monk, and went into the forest. He sat down quietly under a bodhi tree to meditate.

Siddhartha thought about the palace, his fine clothes and his servants.

And Siddhartha knew that when he had fine clothes and servants, he always wanted more.

And the more he kept wanting, the sadder he became.

Siddhartha thought about the old man, the sick man and the dead man – and how everyone can get old and sick and die at the end of their life.

Siddhartha thought about the monk who had no fine clothes or servants but seemed calm and happy.

And Siddhartha knew that everything in nature changes – day turns into night, buds turn into flowers, trees blossom and die.

Siddhartha had learned important lessons. He had become wise. People called him 'the Buddha'.

The Buddha told others what he had learned. He began to teach them to live good lives. He told them they should speak the truth, never harm others and never steal. He told them to have good thoughts in their minds and to try hard to do good deeds.

Everyone was sad when, at the end of his life, the Buddha died, but they remembered all the things he had taught them.

At Wesak, we go to our temple and listen to stories about the Buddha. We hear about his birth, his life and his death.

As we float our lotus-flower lights on the water, the lights remind us that the Buddha's teaching was like a light to show us the way we should live our lives.

I enjoy being with my family and friends at Wesak!

Can you tell a story about Wesak?

Published by Religious and Moral Education Press, A division of SCM-Canterbury Press Ltd, St Mary's Works, St Mary's Plain, Norwich, Norfolk NR3 3BH

Copyright © 2000 Lynne Broadbent and John Logan. Lynne Broadbent and John Logan have asserted their right under the Copyright, Designs and Patents Act, 1988, to be identified as Authors of this Work.

All rights reserved. First published 2000. ISBN 1 85175 204 8

Designed and typeset by Topics – The Creative Partnership, Exeter. Printed in Great Britain by Brightsea Press, Exeter for SCM-Canterbury Press Ltd, Norwich